# Developmental Editing for Non-Fiction

Claire Beveridge

First published in the UK in 2023 by
Chartered Institute of Editing and Proofreading
8 Devonshire Square
London
EC2M 4YJ

# ciep.uk

Copyright © 2023 Chartered Institute of Editing and Proofreading

978 1 915141 14 9 (print)
978 1 915141 15 6 (PDF ebook)

All rights reserved. No part of this publication may be reproduced or used in any manner without written permission from the publisher, except for quoting brief passages in a review.

The moral rights of the author have been asserted.

The information in this work is accurate and current at the time of publication to the best of the author's and publisher's knowledge, but it has been written as a short summary or introduction only. Readers are advised to take further steps to ensure the correctness, sufficiency or completeness of this information for their own purposes.

Development editing, copyediting and proofreading by CIEP members, including Julia Sandford-Cooke, Liz Dalby, Harriet Power, Abi Saffrey and Llinos Edwards.

Typeset in-house
Original design by Ave Design (**avedesignstudio.com**)
Creative commons images from Pexels

# Contents

| | | |
|---|---|---|
| 1 \| | Introduction | 1 |
| | The focus of this guide | 1 |
| 2 \| | What is developmental editing? | 3 |
| | What do non-fiction developmental editors work on? | 6 |
| 3 \| | Working as a non-fiction developmental editor | 7 |
| | What experience or background do you need? | 7 |
| | Advantages of working as a developmental editor | 8 |
| | Disadvantages of working as a developmental editor | 8 |
| | Pathways to developmental editing and finding work | 9 |
| | Working for individuals | 13 |
| | Pricing the project | 17 |
| 4 \| | Managing working relationships | 18 |
| | People skills | 18 |
| | Project and time management skills | 20 |
| 5 \| | The main process of developmental editing | 23 |
| | Suggested workflow | 23 |
| | Establishing the brief | 24 |
| | Conducting a rough read | 26 |
| | Working on the specifics | 27 |
| 6 \| | Writing an editorial report | 36 |

| 7 | Writing a content outline or book proposal | 40 |

    Subject research    41
    Audience profile    41
    Market potential    42

| 8 | Checklist of details to look out for | 43 |

    Abbreviations and consistency of terminology    44
    Presentation of data    44
    Figures and tables    44
    Citations    45
    Biased or insensitive language    45
    Potential legal or ethical issues    45

| 9 | Resources | 46 |

    Books and guides    46
    CIEP fact sheets and focus papers    47
    Courses    47
    Mentoring    48
    Blogs    48
    Webinars    49

# 1 | Introduction

This guide is for editors who want to learn more about developmental editing of non-fiction resources. It introduces the skills involved and practical approaches that they can use, whether they are employed by a publisher or working on a freelance basis. The purpose of this guide is to explain:

- what developmental editing is
- what working as a non-fiction developmental editor involves
- how to manage working relationships
- things to establish before you start
- how to approach developmental editing of a non-fiction manuscript (with a suggested workflow)
- how to write an editorial report
- how to write a content outline or book proposal.

The guide also includes a checklist of details to look out for.

## The focus of this guide

This guide focuses on the process of getting a work of non-fiction into good order before it moves on to the copyediting phase. Depending on the project, developmental editing can take place at different points.

A publisher might seek to commission a work and request that an editor put together a content outline for an author to develop into a complete manuscript, or they may have received a manuscript from an author that needs considerable work before it can be considered ready to move into the production process, either to align it to an existing family of titles or because the flow and structure of the content is disjointed.

Developmental editing may also be requested by an author before they submit their work for consideration by an agent, publisher or journal (if an academic research paper) in order to maximise the chances of it being accepted. A self-publisher may want help to refine the structure and organisation of their content. Alternatively, if the text is an academic work, it might have already been rejected by one publisher and the author may be looking to improve it before it is submitted elsewhere.

How much developmental editing is needed will vary from one work to another, and can be influenced by the wishes of the client (whether it is a publisher or the author) and the author's writing experience. The client may request that you do some or all of the following:

- produce a report that summarises your recommendations
- mark in your suggestions as comments
- make direct changes to the text and move things around.

This guide introduces the things that you need to consider when developmentally editing non-fiction at all levels.

# 2 | What is developmental editing?

The main purpose of developmental editing, as with all editing stages, is to help an author clarify their message and deliver it to the intended audience in the most effective way. Key components of this are determining what the text is trying to achieve, why the reader should care, and identifying the needs of the intended audience and how the text can be made more 'reader-friendly'. If a text is unable to engage its intended audience, it is not going to be successful in conveying the information that it contains.

In the traditional publishing workflow, developmental editing of a manuscript comes after a text has been written and before copyediting, typesetting, proofreading and publication. However, development can also involve the production of book proposals and content outlines, long before the author starts writing (see **chapter 7** 'Writing a content outline or book proposal'), and the first draft of a text may require the addition of significant amounts of content or even a complete re-think. As a result, developmental editing can be involved at three points in the process of bringing a text to publication, as shown below.

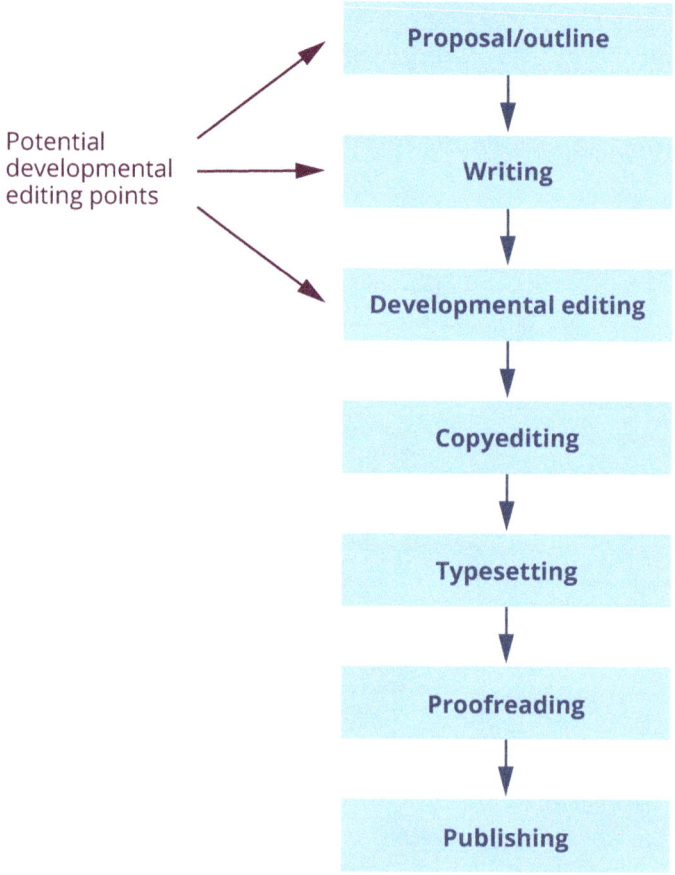

In contrast to line/copyediting and proofreading, where the main focus is at the sentence or word level and on the detail of the text, developmental editing focuses on the bigger picture. Rather than looking at the construction and accuracy of individual sentences, and whether grammar and punctuation are correct, a developmental editor looks at the content, structure, clarity, tone and flow of the text as a whole, judging whether content should be moved from one chapter to another or individual chapters should be restructured (see **chapter 5** 'The main process of developmental editing' for details). If a text contains a lot of writing errors (such as spelling mistakes) at the developmental stage, the developmental editor will leave them for the copyeditor to deal with later on.

In fiction, developmental editing considers the development of the narrative arc: the path the story follows or the sequence of events that happen. It provides a backbone for the story by establishing a clear beginning, middle and end. The development of non-fiction involves a similar process; the editor makes sure that everything hangs together off a central argument or main point, that the argument or point develops in a logical way, that it is appropriately backed up by evidence, and that information is being delivered in a way that will connect with the intended audience. The editor may make or recommend changes that will alter large sections of content and the way in which the information is organised.

Although some developmental editing jobs may involve the editor writing sections of new material, this should not be done to the extent that the text essentially becomes ghostwritten (ie written by someone other than the named author or authors, and who does not receive credit for their writing). Equally, book coaching and developmental editing are not the same. A book coach works with an author while they develop their manuscript and provides guidance and support throughout the whole process, from start to finish. The focus is on working with the author rather than on the content and structure of the manuscript itself.

Confusingly, developmental editing is sometimes called content, substantive, structural or comprehensive editing. The term 'substantive editing' is also used by some to describe what may be called 'line editing', where elements of the text are tightened up and clarified at the chapter, paragraph and sentence levels. Some editors include line editing in their developmental editing service, while others consider it to be a distinct type of editing. Each editor's approach is different, and taking the time to define exactly what each of your services includes and to ensure that your clients understand the differences between them can prevent problems further down the line. This guide considers the key elements of developmental and substantive editing together so that you have a broad overview and can decide what you will offer.

## What do non-fiction developmental editors work on?

Non-fiction developmental editing can be applied to a wide variety of types of work. Some examples are:

- trade non-fiction books for a general readership
- instruction manuals, reports, financial statements and guides
- academic and educational resources and textbooks
- research papers being submitted to journals
- grant proposals and funding reports
- self-published works
- business books and marketing material (eg lead magnets, e-books, promotional brochures or leaflets)
- web content.

Although the items in the list above will differ widely depending on the intended audience, purpose and required tone, the principles that are applied during developmental editing are the same.

# 3 | Working as a non-fiction developmental editor

## What experience or background do you need?

Some experience as a copyeditor is useful before you start taking on developmental editing work because it will give you a good understanding of the editorial process and core principles. The process involves an element of instinct and judgement, and can be quite subjective. For this reason, many non-fiction developmental editors have experience gained from in-house editing at a publishing company, from copywriting, or from critiquing or teaching writing. Alternatively, they may have begun as a freelance copyeditor and/or proofreader and moved into developmental editing over time.

Subject matter expertise is not essential but can be helpful. For example, developmental editors may be former academic researchers, may have previously worked or published in the field being covered (particularly useful if they will be dealing with educational resources), or may have read large volumes of that type of work during their career and may be familiar with any common conventions (this is particularly applicable to specialist fields such as law, finance, science and medicine). In any of the above fields, staying up to date with developments and/or attending relevant conferences can give you added credibility and confidence.

> **Subject matter expertise is not essential but can be helpful.**

## Advantages of working as a developmental editor

Because of the nature of developmental editing, it can be more intellectually engaging than copyediting and proofreading. Depending on how well a text is written and whether the topic concerned is within your direct area of expertise, the development of a project may be a genuine cognitive workout, a bit like solving a puzzle. For this reason, it tends to be the most lucrative of the services that editors offer. It is also arguably more creative, and the process of improving disjointed manuscripts and confusing arguments can be deeply satisfying. Another benefit is that you may develop long-term and meaningful relationships with clients (eg with authors at the start of their writing careers).

> *... the process of improving disjointed manuscripts and confusing arguments can be deeply satisfying.*

## Disadvantages of working as a developmental editor

The flip side is that, depending on the task, developmental editing can be very time-consuming. Research time needs to be factored in so that you can tackle a text with confidence and provide clients with the best advice. Some texts may need a large amount of work, and it can be difficult to decipher what the author is trying to say. The author or client may also turn out to be resistant to the changes you suggest, so to some extent you need a thick skin; it can be demoralising if you have spent days working on a text only for your carefully thought-out suggestions to be rejected. In some cases you will be right, but it is also important to be open-minded to the fact that you may be wrong, and to remember that it is the author's book, not yours. The old editing adage 'leave well enough alone' applies, and this can be difficult to judge; sometimes you may feel tempted to intervene when it is not really necessary because this is a higher-level edit and you want to justify your rate. Ensuring that the brief is clear and taking the time to meet with all of the parties involved before you start editing can help to avoid some of the issues described above.

## Pathways to developmental editing and finding work

There is no single pathway to developmental editing. There is a lack of specialist training available for developmental editing of non-fiction, and for this reason many editors come to it by learning 'on the job' once they have some experience as a copyeditor or proofreader. Some publishers will advertise vacancies for developmental editors. If your application is successful, you may find yourself involved in the research, commissioning and development of a list of titles with limited supervision or mentoring, although whether the developmental or commissioning editor is responsible for these aspects can differ between publishers. Another route, particularly if you have an academic background or a particular subject specialism, is to apply to work for a service that develops academic research papers before they are submitted to a journal.

These usually provide some element of training and detailed feedback on your work, and so can be a useful place to start.

Alternatives include offering to put together a content outline or book proposal, or to conduct a rough read of a manuscript and put together a summary of the work needed, if you are employed by a publisher. Alternatively, if you are working for a publisher on a freelance basis, are undertaking a copyedit and notice developmental issues, you could try one of two approaches. You could contact the publisher early on to let them know the issues that you have identified and ask whether they would like to extend the scope of the task to developmental editing, or you could note the issues in the email when you return the work, make suggestions (but do not make any developmental changes without getting permission first) and let them know that you would be happy to discuss doing some developmental work for them. Another option is to approach someone you know who subcontracts developmental editing and ask whether you could take on some tasks. These can all help you to hone your developmental instincts and begin to develop a portfolio.

Networking with other editors is a useful way of getting referrals, as is noting that you offer developmental editing wherever you have profiles that advertise your availability for work (such as the CIEP Directory and LinkedIn). Some editing organisations offer mentoring programmes enabling you to get one-to-one support from an experienced editor (see the **Resources** section for details). If you are looking to work with independent (also known as 'indie') authors who are self-publishing, it is worth applying to join an organisation such as the Alliance of Independent Authors as a Partner Member.

> **Networking with other editors is a useful way of getting referrals.**

## Working for publishers

### Traditional publishers

Traditional publishers can be categorised according to the types of book that they publish:

- Educational publishers create books and learning materials for use by students and teachers or lecturers, usually with a specific syllabus in mind.
- Academic and professional publishers create materials for professionals who need access to reliable, up-to-date information about best practice or standards, for example healthcare professionals or lawyers.
- Trade publishers create materials that are aimed at a more general readership and that are mostly sold through traditional channels, like bookshops.

If you are working for a traditional publisher, there are generally two types of task that you may work on:

*Researching potential titles and putting together content outlines*

This can involve competitor analysis, research on the intended topic and investigation of the current needs of the intended audience. Assessment of whether publishing on the proposed topic is likely to be worthwhile may also be included. If it has already been established that there is a viable market for the book, you may be asked to provide a content outline that will act as a framework for what the text will contain and how it will be structured, which the author will develop and flesh out (**chapter 7** 'Writing a content outline or book proposal' has more detail). If you are working for a trade publisher, you may need to liaise with someone in the marketing team about the manuscript's content, as well as with the editor responsible for publishing the manuscript.

*Developing a manuscript that has been submitted by an author*

If a content outline was approved before the author started work, you will need to check whether the main points have been covered by the manuscript to avoid problems later on. In addition to the general process of developmental editing, you may also need to ensure that the text adheres to a particular template that the publisher will provide or adapt it to fit the style of a series of books.

## Companies that offer research journal services

Some publishers of research journals offer developmental editing services. You are likely to work as part of a team of editors, each with a different role. As a developmental editor, you will be asked to examine the content in detail, make strategic comments and suggestions, and compile a report summarising the key issues. Usually, at least one experienced editor will then conduct their own review for quality assurance, and you will receive feedback on what you have done.

## Working for individuals

Doing developmental editing for individuals is very different to undertaking it for a publisher. Publishers usually have established styles and processes that they will ask you to follow. Individuals rarely have such things in place, unless they have had clear guidance from a journal or publisher regarding expectations and requirements, and you will need to invest some time in assessing and connecting with the author before you start working on their text. Some authors will seek out the help of a developmental editor to increase the chances of their manuscript being accepted by a traditional publisher or agent, asking them to work on the finished manuscript and/or help put together a book proposal (see **chapter 7** 'Writing a content outline or book proposal'). Others will be independent authors who are self-publishing and want to refine the structure and organisation of their content.

### Understanding the author's problems before you start

It is always worth taking the time to liaise with the author before you begin editing, for example via an email, online video or telephone conversation, or by asking them to complete a questionnaire. As well as enabling you to establish a good working relationship with them, an understanding of any problems that the author may have and their views on the project can prove invaluable later on when considering whether the text is meeting its aims. Authors may struggle to get detailed, honest and objective feedback from colleagues, friends/family and peers, and it is vital that they view you as fulfilling this role, rather than interfering with or corrupting their 'magnum opus'.

As far as the author is concerned, the stakes can be high, and understanding their ambitions and any pressures they are under can help you establish a good rapport with them. Although some non-academic authors may be writing for personal satisfaction, they may be creating marketing material or writing a book or e-book that they hope will make them money. It is now common for businesses and entrepreneurs to produce lead magnets (a marketing tool, often in the form of a workbook or guide, that is usually made available for free in exchange for a potential customer's contact information) and business books as part of their marketing strategies.

For academic authors, the advancement of their careers can depend on their ability to get work published. Some research journals and publishers are also more prestigious than others, and the quality of a manuscript will affect not only the chances of it getting published, but whether it is accepted by a high- or low-ranking journal. Some authors may already have had their manuscript rejected by one journal or publisher and may be looking to improve it before submitting it somewhere else.

## Assessing the work and the author

Different authors have varying needs, and it can be worth being flexible about what you offer. For example, offering to write a report summarising your recommendations rather than making changes to the text may appeal to an author with a limited budget (see **chapter 6** 'Writing an editorial report' for more detail). This may also be more suitable for authors who have more experience of the editing process, and who can take general feedback and apply it to the manuscript as a whole. Others may benefit from extra assistance.

Authors in the early stages of their writing careers may be unfamiliar with the publishing process and the different types of editing service available. Explain what the various stages of editing involve and clearly set out what your developmental editing service does and does not include early on in the discussion process. Include in the contract a description of the work that will be done, how many revisions will be included, and details of any limitations or disclaimers (such as the final work being the author's responsibility and that you cannot be held liable if their work is rejected or fails to become a bestseller).

It is also a good idea to gauge how receptive the author is likely to be to you recommending significant changes and to having to make major revisions to their text. Some authors may not welcome your suggestions, while others may assume that the majority of their work is done once their manuscript is passed to an editor. However, the developmental editing process may identify that content is missing or that large sections need to be reworked. The author may not have factored this possibility into the timescale that they have in mind.

# "Different authors have varying needs, and it can be worth being flexible about what you offer."

Some authors may have unrealistic expectations about what you can do for them. For example, a scientist may have had their research paper rejected by a journal and may think that you will be able to shape it into something brilliant, when actually the problems are more to do with the research that was conducted, the way the data were analysed and the conclusions made. This emphasises the importance of both looking at the text before you agree to do a piece of work and setting out exactly what will and will not be covered.

Other authors may be under the impression that having some sections of their text developmentally edited but not others, for example to save money, is a worthwhile approach. In such situations, further discussion may help them to understand the importance of having the whole text reviewed to ensure overall consistency and coherence. A desire for a cheap service could indicate that the author may not be willing to invest what is needed for their text to reach its full potential.

The following questions may be useful when assessing the author:

- How much writing experience do they have and what experience do they have of the publishing process?
- How much do they know about the editing process and the different types of editing?
- Who do they consider the book to be for and what do they consider the central argument to be?

- Are their expectations realistic regarding what you can do for them in terms of changes and recommendations?
- Are the timescale and budget that they have in mind realistic?
- Are they likely to be open to making significant changes and investing the time and effort to do this if needed?

For all of the points described above it is important to trust your instincts. If you have qualms about taking on a project for any reason, it may be best to politely decline it. Some tips for handling relationships with clients can be found in **chapter 4** 'Managing working relationships'.

As a side note, it is unethical to developmentally edit dissertations and theses. How well the author can describe and analyse their work forms part of the assessment for their degree, and most universities have strict rules regarding what is allowed. While proofreading is acceptable (ideally always with the approval of the student's supervisor), making substantial changes is not (further guidance can be found in the CIEP guide *Proofreading Theses and Dissertations* by Stephen Cashmore).

## Pricing the project

Publishers are most likely to offer work set at predetermined rates, and it will be up to you to judge whether or not the rate offered is reasonable. If you are working directly with an author there is usually more flexibility and you can tailor your quote to their needs. Ask to see a sample of the text, preferably the whole manuscript but at least one chapter, and consider the following questions:

- How well-written does the manuscript appear to be?
- Does the text have a coherent structure?
- Are there any obvious issues?
- To what extent do issues affect the text (ie are there only a few or are there lots of major ones)?
- Is the brief realistic regarding the timescale, budget and what you are required to do?
- How many rounds of revisions will be needed?
- Does the publisher or author want you to produce an editorial report?

In addition to the questions above, you need to consider your likely rate of work (which is easier to estimate once you have some experience of developmental editing; keeping a record of the time spent on projects is good practice for exactly this reason), current market rates, and additional considerations such as office costs, pension provision and insurance (see the CIEP guide *Pricing a Project: How to prepare a professional quotation* by Melanie Thompson for detailed advice). It is then up to you whether you incorporate into your quotation a rate based on word count or estimated hours.

It is normal for the rates charged for developmental editing to be higher than those for copyediting (see the current CIEP recommended minimum rate as an example). Every editor is different and there is no right or wrong way to settle on a price. The amount you charge can also be influenced by the extent of your experience and whether you are working on a project that requires specialist knowledge or skills.

# 4 | Managing working relationships

## People skills

Imagine that you have lived in a house for many years and that the garden is your pride and joy. Every weekend is spent diligently tending to it, and you have lots of different species of unusual plants. Now imagine that you have had to put the house on the market and you overhear a potential buyer remark, 'Let's put an offer in, but we'll need to rip the garden out and start again ... it's awful.' How do you think you would feel?

Authors are often described as treating their manuscripts like their babies. It is therefore understandable that they can be uncomfortable with the idea that changes need to be made and that they can become defensive if they feel overly criticised. For this reason, a key skill of developmental editors is the ability to earn an author's trust and encourage a sense of collaboration.

It is important to remember to praise the author's efforts as well as give suggestions for improvement. Making an effort to sound enthusiastic about a project and stating your commitment to helping the author make their text the best it can be will pay dividends in the long run. If an author is uncooperative when they receive your feedback, it may be that they do not fully understand what is involved at the developmental stage and what this process seeks to achieve. Part of your role as a developmental editor is to coach the author towards producing a better text, and emphasising that it can be an interactive process where you will work together to arrive at the best outcome can break down barriers. Scheduling a meeting or call where you can discuss suggestions and explore ideas together can be particularly helpful for both parties, and can save hours of emailing back and forth.

Effective comments and queries can make or break the development of a manuscript. The questions that you are asking need to be clear, with the reasons behind them explained. It is also worth making the effort to provide detailed explanations of why any major changes are needed, so that the author understands their importance and likely impact. Useful approaches when writing comments and queries include:

- Providing the author with two examples to choose from, rather than asking an open-ended question. For example, 'What do you mean here?' is less likely to yield a specific answer than 'Would "X" or "Y" be better here?'
- Avoiding the word 'you' in comments and referring to the reader instead – for example, 'Is the reader likely to be familiar with this term?' or 'This could confuse the reader because …'
- Playing devil's advocate (and depending on your relationship with the author, potentially making it clear that you are deliberately doing this) or asking questions that might seem obvious or silly in an attempt to find the right solution – for example, 'Do these two terms mean the same thing and, if not, are less-knowledgeable readers likely to know the difference?'
- Modelling how you want the author to write something in the comments and then adding 'Please could you write more like this?' or providing potential solutions to issues by example.
- Wondering 'out loud' whether something is a good option or a problem, rather than telling the author that it is.

Although developmental editors need to be tactful, sometimes they need to hold their ground. If the project has been commissioned by a publisher, the word count requirements and content outline may support your case if you and the author disagree; however, if the author is a self-publisher, you may not have such tools to back up your arguments. If the scope of the project allows (and it is a commissioned text), expert readers or reviewers can be brought in to give their opinions. This can lend weight to your advice, but can also backfire if the reviewer has their own agenda or conflicting opinions.

In extreme cases, if you cannot overcome the problems in a text or if the working relationship breaks down, it may be necessary to walk away from a project, but it is also important to have the humility to accept that the author may be right. At the end of the day, it is the author's book, not yours, and if they are adamant that things should stay the way they are, that may be the end of the matter.

## Project and time management skills

Developmental editors need good time and project management skills. Projects can easily be knocked off schedule if the process identifies that the author needs to provide new content or that there are issues that need to be addressed, or if deadlines further down the chain are missed. This can have significant effects on your cash flow and on your own work schedule if you are fully booked.

Being able to effectively and flexibly manage your time, while keeping an eye on the project's key deadlines, is essential (see the CIEP guide *Editorial Project Management* by Abi Saffrey for advice). When estimating how long things will take, review at least one sample of the text and consider how much really needs to be done. It is worth deliberately overestimating, because many developmental edits can seem relatively straightforward at first glance but have significant issues upon closer inspection. It is also good practice to build in time to allow for things to go wrong if you can.

Having a clear brief and a contract in place is key if scope creep (changes to or growth of a project once it has started) is to be avoided. Try to be as comprehensive as possible about what will and will not be covered when agreeing the brief and contract. If the publisher or author starts to ask you to do additional tasks, have a conversation before you do them so that you do not end up doing more work than was initially agreed for the same fee. You could suggest that they pay you more or change the workflow and/or responsibilities.

Being proactive with communication can prevent problems from developing. Do not assume that someone involved in the project knows what they should be doing and when. Check with them, and make sure that all agreements made are recorded and circulated to those involved. A useful technique to prevent things being missed is to use the RACI (responsible, accountable, consulted and informed) model to clarify the roles of individuals at different stages of a project:

- **Responsible:** Directly responsible for something being completed.
- **Accountable:** Has final authority regarding successful completion (ie the buck stops here).
- **Consulted:** Has insight that should feed into the process.
- **Informed:** Not directly involved but should be kept up to speed.

A RACI chart for part of a project involving a trade publisher and a freelance editor might look like this:

|  | Publisher staff member | Author | Developmental editor | Marketing team member |
|---|---|---|---|---|
| Development of content outline | Accountable | Consulted | Responsible | Consulted |
| Manuscript writing | Accountable | Responsible | Informed | Informed |
| Developmental edit | Accountable | Consulted | Responsible | Informed |

If problems start to arise that may affect the project, everyone concerned should be made aware of them as early as possible. Risk management is better than dealing with a last-minute crisis. Diarising dates on which you will contact the author to check on progress can help stop a project from slipping and (if circulated with the author at the start of the project) can give them some accountability, as can sending them key dates well in advance and asking them to block out periods of time to work on amendments. If the publishing schedule changes for any reason, update the author as soon as possible.

Keeping good records is essential. You want to ensure that files such as manuscript documents and contracts are organised in a sensible way, and that you keep a record of email conversations. Back up files regularly, either using an internet-based system (such as Dropbox or OneDrive) or locally (a hard drive, a USB stick or another computer), and use a clear file-naming system for version control.

# 5 | The main process of developmental editing

## Suggested workflow

There are many ways to approach developmental editing of non-fiction texts, but a common workflow is outlined below. Different editors vary in their approach. Some conduct a rough read before tackling specifics, whereas others dive straight in. Time and budget constraints often do not allow for a third pass through a text, but if they do it is worth doing a final read-through to check for anything that you might have missed and that your suggestions make sense.

1. **Establish the brief.** Make sure that you are clear about the scope of the work to be undertaken and what the publisher and/or author is expecting. If the text needs to adhere to a particular template or fit the style of a series of books, check the instructions.
2. **First pass: rough read.** At this stage, you are looking to gain a general impression of the central argument or main point, and to identify any conflicting arguments or major issues. It is also an opportunity to get a feel for whether the manuscript is coherent overall and to identify any obviously missing content.
3. **Second pass: work on the specifics.** Examine the content, structure, clarity, tone and flow of the text in detail.
4. **Third pass: final check.** If making changes directly to the text, check the overall flow on the basis of the changes made and that everything is consistent. This may be a skim-read if time is tight.
5. **Write an editorial report.** If required, put together a report summarising the main issues in the text and your suggestions for their resolution.

## Establishing the brief

Because of the nature of developmental editing, it is essential that both you and your clients have a clear understanding of the work that will be undertaken before you start. Considering the fact that even editors can struggle to agree on where developmental editing ends and line/copyediting starts, it is important that you set out what your service will and will not include, and that you have the client sign a contract confirming that they agree to the terms of both parties and the scope of the work. Ask to see the text before you commit to working on a project and agree a fee. The speed at which you will be able to work through the text will depend on its complexity, the extent of any issues, and whether you are making changes directly to the text or only making comments and suggestions. Also take the time to discuss the project with the author. This helps you gauge what their needs are and how receptive they are likely to be to you making significant changes to their work.

Important things to consider include:

- Who is the intended audience? Once you know this, consider the style of delivery that will be most appropriate for them (eg will they expect and respond best to a formal, academic tone or less formal language) and how you can make the text more reader-friendly.
- What is the purpose of the text? Is it trying to persuade the reader to take action or to come around to the author's point of view?
- Will any line/copyediting be included?
- Does the author or publisher expect you to write a report to accompany the manuscript?
- Is the author or publisher happy for you to make major structural changes, or do they prefer that you make recommendations in the form of comments or as a report?
- What book is the publisher trying to publish, and does it align with the author's agenda and interests?
- Is the timeline clear and reasonable for all steps in the process and everyone involved? Who is responsible for each step in the process and when do they need to do them by? Are there any tasks that are dependent on a previous one being completed before it is begun, and is this understood by all parties involved?
- If working with a publisher, who is the key contact and who is responsible for the project management side of things (how often you will have progress discussions and what form such meetings will take, milestones if appropriate, etc)?
- It is also important that you get a sense of how committed the publisher is to producing the book, and who has the final say on content. Do they have an 'at the end of the day, it's the author's book' attitude, or do they consider that the author must write the book that the publisher has envisioned?
- Does the text need to adhere to a particular template or will it be part of an existing series of titles? If the answer is yes, make sure that you have been sent all of the relevant style information. If applicable and the manuscript is in the form of an MS Word file, has the necessary template been attached?

It is possible that the project may become delayed for any number of reasons, or that the developmental edit will identify major problems that need to be addressed before the text can progress through the publishing process. If this happens, be proactive in revising the plan and recirculating it to anyone likely to be affected.

## Conducting a rough read

Some developmental editors prefer not to conduct an initial rough read and instead wade straight in, but reading through the text with an open mind can be a useful way of gaining a general impression of the text as a whole. Identifying major issues early on can help you focus your efforts in the most effective way, and there may an opportunity for the author to address them before you spend too much time working on the detail of the manuscript.

When conducting a rough read, it can be helpful to make brief notes on the following:

- Is there a central argument or main point, and is it clear?
- If there are several different arguments competing for the reader's attention, do any of these contradict each other?
- Does the text fulfil its intended purpose?
- Is the text written in such a way that it will connect with the intended audience?
- Is there anything obviously missing? This includes checking that everything in the content outline has been covered, if one is available.
- Are there any significant changes in style and/or tone?
- Are there any sections that repeat each other?
- Depending on the intended audience, are there any issues in terms of the use of jargon or slang?
- Is any of the content or terminology used likely to be considered inflammatory or offensive?

## Working on the specifics

At this stage of the process, the emphasis should be on refining the content, structure, clarity, tone and flow of the text. Although each is discussed separately below, in reality there can be considerable overlap between them.

### Content

*What is the central argument?*

In general, every text should have a central argument or main point that is logical and persuasive, and the text as a whole should hang off it and support it. For example, the central argument could be the reasons why a consumer's life will be better if they purchase a product, how particular life events shaped the career of a historical figure, or the implications of new research findings for our understanding of a disease. Many texts that have developmental issues contain too many subjects. Some texts will work well with several different points or themes being covered in parallel, but they all need to be brought together eventually and their relationships with each other explained.

Unless you have had a very clear steer from the publisher or author, you may need to decipher what the text actually should be about and seek agreement before you adjust the content accordingly. If you are struggling to identify the central argument, it can help to work through the text systematically:

1. Use a different indicator for each subject or idea, whether a code, symbol or description, whatever you find easiest. For example, in a medical text you might use 'causes/CAU', 'symptoms/SYMP', 'signs/SIGN', 'diagnosis/DIAG', 'treatment/TRT', 'follow-up/FUP' and 'outcomes/OUT'. Next, read through the text and create a list outlining each time the subject or idea changes, and the relevant page number.
2. Once you have been through the whole text, review the list to identify the subject that is covered the most and any that can be grouped together.

3. Any subjects that seem unrelated to the majority of the content should be flagged, either for removal because they distract from the text's main point or for further work from the author.

If you judge the number of subjects in the text to be a major issue, discuss the matter with the publisher and/or author before you go much further. Put forward several suggestions for which subject should be the central argument (explaining your reasoning, eg are any particularly novel?), and seek agreement on which is best considering the intended audience.

Once you have clarity on what the central argument is, check whether it is supported by the table of contents. If not, how can the table of contents be revised? Would it benefit from rearrangement, different chapter headings, or some content being added or deleted? There may be limits to what you can do if the text is part of a series that follows an established structure and style.

*Does the manuscript meet its objectives?*

Once you have identified the central argument, evaluate whether the manuscript meets its objectives in its current form. For example:

- If the text is a report that needs to convey key findings, are they clearly stated with their significance explained, ideally emphasised in a standalone abstract or summary, or are they buried in large sections of text?
- If created for marketing purposes, does the text have a clear call to action? Has the reader been provided with the information they need to make a decision? Have potential objections been addressed?
- If an instruction manual or guide, has everything been included that the reader needs to know to be successful?
- If the text presents a new theory or thesis, is the reader likely to agree with the central argument once they have read the text?

If the answer to the above questions is 'no', consider why that is. Would the manuscript benefit from additional or less content, is the tone wrong for the intended audience, etc?

*Should any content be added or removed?*

Many texts are too long when they are submitted and benefit from some cuts being made. Sometimes the author is so enthusiastic about the topic that they do not know when to stop, or they may be concerned that they need to include everything that might possibly be relevant for completeness. However, there is a fine balance to be struck between providing sufficient information for the reader to be satisfied and too much, resulting in the reader feeling swamped or, even worse, bored. If you are working for a publisher or the author of a research paper, there may be strict word counts that the author needs to adhere to.

In some instances, as you read through the text, you may come across areas of repetition. Where this occurs, you could recommend merging the relevant sections into a separate chapter or subsection, rather than leaving them distributed throughout the text. Using the systematic process outlined in 'What is the central argument' (above) can help you identify where repetition occurs.

There can also be instances where content needs to be added. For example, in an autobiography, the author might spend a chapter describing the events of a phase in their life without explaining how the circumstances came about. Similarly, in a textbook, the author might fail to consider that some readers may not be specialists in the field; in such a case, including thorough explanations of terminology and approaches (perhaps by adding a glossary if there is not one already) would be helpful.

The following questions can be used to help determine whether content should be added or removed:

- Has the author provided enough evidence to support the central argument?
- Does any information detract from the central argument or fail to support it?
- Does any of the content risk confusing the reader?
- Is any information repeated unnecessarily?
- Are any claims made that are not sufficiently backed up?
- Has enough background information been provided to prevent the reader from being confused as to why things are relevant or important?
- Has the author assumed that the reader has more background knowledge about the subject than is likely, or do they risk patronising the reader by including too much explanation?
- Has the author provided enough information to keep a specialist reader interested?
- If an educational text, has enough information been provided for the student to know what is required by the specification/syllabus?
- Has the author provided content that will hook in a reader who would otherwise be uninterested in reading a text on the subject?

## Structure

A manuscript should be structured in a way that supports the flow of the text and the development of the central argument.

### Chapters

Ideally, chapters and the sections within them should build on each other in some way. Each chapter should have a purpose and be arranged in a way that emphasises the rationale. There should be consistency between the different chapters, and if they are going to be broken up into sections through the use of subheadings, the subsections should be similarly structured.

### Paragraphs

As with chapters, each paragraph should have a purpose and should normally focus on one subject or idea. Try to break up paragraphs that contain lots of subjects. The reverse outlining approach described in the section about tone (see page 33) can help you identify if this is a problem.

### Subheadings

Subheadings can be a powerful tool with which to bring order to a text, but care needs to be taken. Depending on the nature of the text, too many subheadings or levels of subheading can negatively affect the flow of text, potentially making each section feel constricted. Conversely, too few subheadings can leave the reader feeling as if they are wading through pages of information with no direction. The solution for any given text depends on the subject matter and whether the text is required to fit an established template. In general, the following rules apply:

- As with chapters, all subheadings should have a purpose.
- Subheadings should divide the text up in a logical way (it is important to check whether each use of heading level is appropriate).
- The use of heading levels should be tiered; for example, each level 2 heading should support the level 1 heading above it.
- A new level of subheading should not be introduced if it is only going to be used once, because it has no real purpose.

*Transitions*

Transitions from one chapter or subheading to the next are also important when considering structure. In general, each chapter should lead into the next in some way, or into forthcoming chapters if the text does not have a linear structure; however, this is not necessarily the case in educational textbooks where chapters might represent standalone units of a course. In some cases, it can be useful to use transitions that act like a cliffhanger would in a fiction book, to hook the reader into reading further. In others, there may simply be a need to ensure that the content of one chapter flows smoothly into the next, without ending or starting abruptly.

## Clarity

In addition to checking that the order in which information is given is logical, you need to consider whether ideas are being articulated clearly. This is when some knowledge of the subject being discussed can be useful. Questions to consider are:

- Are the arguments or the way that information is being presented likely to leave the reader feeling confused, or are they too simplistic?
- Are there elements that just do not add up?
- Is the reader likely to reach the conclusions that the author wants them to on the basis of the information provided?
- Is the way the text is written appropriate for the intended audience?
- Is there unnecessary use of jargon, and if yes, how could the language be simplified?
- Is there unnecessary use of slang, and if yes, how could the language be made more professional?
- Are different terms being used to describe the same thing when one would do?
- Could information be presented more clearly through the use of a figure or table?

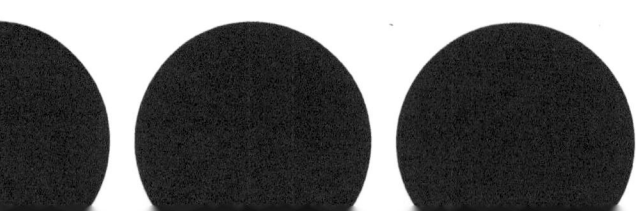

## Tone

The tone of a text relates to the attitude of the author and the feelings that it evokes in the reader. The tone can be affected by the choice of words used, the structures of sentences, and how things are phrased. It is also worth considering whether suggested figures or tables need to be altered. In general, the tone of a text should be consistent throughout. There will be some exceptions to this depending on the nature of the text, but they are rare – for example, in a book where individual chapters have been written by different authors and each chapter should retain its author's voice.

When considering whether the tone used is appropriate, it is important to keep the intended reader in mind. Will they expect or prefer the tone to be formal or informal? Is the current tone too dry or inappropriately jolly? For example, a text written for patients who have just received a serious diagnosis would need to strike a delicate balance between being engaging and encouraging, and realistic and informative. Short sentences with clear, simple explanations of what terms mean would help the reader navigate the information, and would be most likely to be written in the first or second person. Similarly, a formal government report would not use contractions (don't, can't, it's, etc) or chatty or conversational language, would most likely be written in the third person and should come across as authoritative, rather than woolly or aggressive.

> **The tone of a text relates to the attitude of the author and the feelings that it evokes in the reader.**

## Flow

All types of editing are concerned with ensuring that writing flows (ie it reads smoothly from beginning to end). When we talk about improving flow in developmental editing, we are considering the following:

- Is the information structured logically?
- Are there smooth transitions from one section to the next?
- Does the central argument or story develop as the reader moves through the manuscript?
- Can similar ideas be grouped together?

Reverse outlining is a process that can help you check whether the sequence of information makes sense. It is very similar to the process suggested in 'What is the central argument?' (under 'Content' above). If you have already done that, you can skip step 1:

1. Using a different indicator for each subject or idea (either a code or description), read through the text and create a list outlining each time the subject or idea changes, and the relevant page number. This is your reverse outline.
2. Review the list and ask the following questions:
    a. Is the order of the subjects/ideas logical?
    b. Is it clear how each subject/idea connects to the next?
    c. Are there any gaps in the information or the logic presented?
    d. Could the flow be improved by arranging the subjects in a different order?

Many texts will follow a linear sequence (eg a text that describes events chronologically or that takes the reader through different stages in a process). When dealing with a text like this, it can be helpful to sketch out a timeline or a flow diagram as you work through the book, to help you check that the order in which the information is being given makes sense or that events are described in the right sequence. Representing things visually can be a useful strategy, so take the time to devise a method that works for you.

# 5 | The main process of developmental editing

Other texts can seem more diffuse and provide more of a challenge. Useful approaches to try when dealing with diffuse texts include:

- moving from small to large or large to small (eg national to global and vice versa)
- moving from known to new knowledge
- grouping similar ideas together (eg advantages and disadvantages, causes and effects, crimes and punishments, etc)
- following an investigative format: introduction/background, theory/assertion, methods/analytical approach, evidence/results, discussion/reasoning and conclusions.

In some cases, it may be possible to reorganise chapters so that a pattern of themes is encountered in each one, ending with a concluding chapter that brings all the strands together.

**Chapter 1**
Subject 1 (what happened and why), ending with conclusions that will relate to chapter 4

**Chapter 2**
Subject 2 (what happened and why), ending with conclusions that will relate to chapter 4

**Chapter 3**
Subject 3 (what happened and why), ending with conclusions that will relate to chapter 4

**Chapter 4**
The central argument is discussed with all the strands in the preceding chapters brought together and their relevance to each other explained

# 6 | Writing an editorial report

An editorial report is a summary of the major strengths and weaknesses of a text with suggestions for improvement. Reports can be requested by publishers as part of assessing whether to accept a manuscript, or by a service that develops research papers before they are submitted to a journal. They can also be requested by authors so that they can get objective, professional advice that they can implement themselves, which is cheaper than them paying their editor to spend additional time making the changes suggested, and you may be asked to focus on specific concerns if they have them. Although some developmental editors include reports in their service as a matter of course, others offer them as a standalone service.

The contents of an editorial report vary according to the needs of the client, but generally include:

- a summary of the overall findings
- a description of what is working well
- a list of problems with some suggestions for improvement (divided into categories as appropriate)
- a final summary of the key recommendations.

It is worth making notes on problems, dividing them into categories, in a separate file as you read through the text. Creating a pro forma template for your report (or using one supplied by the publisher if applicable) that you can begin to populate as you work through the text, rather than creating the report from scratch once the developmental editing process is complete, can save you a lot of time. A basic template for a report is provided below, followed by a brief example.

| Element | Description |
| --- | --- |
| Summary of text | An opening paragraph summarising the aims of the work, the central argument and who might be interested in the text. If the text is research-based, you might include an assessment of the perceived novelty of the work. |
| Main advice | Describe what is working well before summarising your main advice and the potential benefits if the author follows it. |
| Essential points | Summarise the main points that the author needs to address before the text can be considered fit for publishing. |
| Detailed feedback | This could be a discussion of each chapter or section in turn (eg the introduction, methods, results, discussion and conclusion of a scientific research paper). It should include commentary on the text's overall organisation and flow, with any suggestions for improvement, and mention of any other issues that the author should be aware of. |

*Summary of text*

This book describes [describe subject area]. Although a number of books have been published on this topic in recent years, they have not addressed the [central argument] presented in this text/resolved the issue discussed by the [central argument]. A book that addresses the [central argument] is therefore likely to be of interest, and the success of previous titles in this area suggests that this book has the potential to appeal to a wide readership.

*Main advice*

The central argument is persuasive, and sufficient evidence is provided to support the claims on which it is based. However, the development of the central argument is disjointed throughout the book to the extent that the relevance of some findings is unclear where they are mentioned. This is likely to make it difficult for some readers to follow the central argument. There is also heavy use of jargon. Given that the intended audience is first-year university students, simplifying the language used and providing clear and consistent definitions would make it easier for some readers to navigate the text.

*Essential points*

- The flow of the central argument through the text is disjointed. I suggest revising the order in which the information is presented so that the central argument develops in a logical way as the reader moves through the book.
- The language could be revised to use plain English so that it would be more suitable for the intended audience. Careful review of terminology used is recommended to avoid unnecessary jargon and ensure that simple definitions are provided, and it is worth considering including a glossary of terms. There are some instances where more than one term has been used for the same thing, which could confuse the reader.

- The opening chapter would be strengthened by clearly summarising what has already been covered by other books in this field and the new angle that this book contributes (without spelling out exactly what it is because you want to hook the reader in to read the whole book).

*Detailed feedback*

[Discussion of each chapter or section in turn, outlining problems and recommendations relating to content, structure, clarity, tone and flow. Any other issues that you want to draw the author's attention to should be mentioned here.]

You may also choose to add brief annotations to the manuscript as you read through it, but only to draw the author's attention to issues and without the level of detail that would be expected in a full edit.

Companies that offer developmental editing of research papers before they are submitted to a target journal often require their editors to produce editorial reports to accompany annotated papers, but they can be requested in isolation. The reports aim to summarise the main problems and opportunities of the paper, and may also suggest some suitable and realistic journals for submission. The company usually provides a template for the report and suggestions for presenting feedback to ensure consistency between freelancers. If the service deals with scientific and medical papers, the report is usually divided into the sections that are conventional in those fields (abstract, introduction, methods, results, discussion, conclusion: see the CIEP guide *Editing Scientific and Medical Research Articles* by Claire Bacon for more detail). In some cases, you may be asked to differentiate your suggestions into 'desirable' and 'essential' issues for the author to address.

# 7 | Writing a content outline or book proposal

Content outlines and book proposals can take a variety of forms. A content outline generally includes a brief summary of the topic that the text will cover and the central argument, and proposes how the final book will be structured, so acts as a framework for the book as it is written. Content outlines usually include the table of contents and a brief summary of what each chapter will contain. They may also include information about knowledge gaps in the field that the book will cover and an assessment of the text's market potential.

A book proposal is more detailed and sets out to convince a publisher that a book is worth publishing. Book proposals usually contain the following:

- A brief summary of the topic that the text will cover and the central argument.
- A sample chapter or chapters: these should ideally give a sense of the overall writing style, and include the chapter or chapters that most effectively introduce the central argument and the author's analysis of it.
- A biography of the author, with the aim of persuading the publisher that they are perfectly placed to write the book.
- An analysis of competing and/or existing titles.
- A description of the target audience.
- A marketing plan: this should set out steps that the author will take to market the book, summarise any useful connections that the author has, and indicate the size of their audience (ie the number of people on the email mailing list or the sales figures of a previous title).
- Any additional information, such as the expected word count or relevant statistics.

If you are tasked with putting together a content outline or book proposal, there are three key things that you need to consider: subject research, audience profile and market potential.

## Subject research

Proposing what information needs to be included in the book can be a balancing act. If you do not provide enough detail, the outline or proposal is unlikely to be approved; however, if you provide too much, the author will be restricted in how they can develop the text. This can become problematic if the author is being employed because they are an expert in the field. If in doubt about the level of detail required, ask the publisher to provide examples of previous successful outlines, particularly if the text will be part of a family of titles. Although you do not need to be a specialist in the subject that the text will cover, you will need to spend enough time familiarising yourself with it for you to write with confidence.

## Audience profile

Taking the time to develop a picture of the intended reader, by thinking about questions like the ones below, can help you ensure that the book conveys its information effectively:

- Who is the main readership and how do they like to receive information?
- Are there any other potential audiences and how can the text be made to appeal to them?
- What is going to hook the reader in and is there anything that is likely to alienate them?
- What are the needs of the intended audience and how can the text be tailored to meet them – for example, are they busy professionals that are already knowledgeable about the topic being covered but need an easily navigated summary of best practice, or are they someone who needs a broad range of background information to persuade them of the topic's importance and/or galvanise them to take action?

## Market potential

If you are working for a publisher, you may need to liaise with a member of the marketing team. They may be able to provide you with information about the market and other relevant information (ie how the book will be pitched, whether it is being launched at the same time as an event or to accompany something else, etc). Considering the following questions may also be useful:

- Are there already other titles in the field?
- How will the text compete with other titles in the field and what is its unique selling point?
- How will the text be made topical and/or current?

If you are working for a publisher, and the text will be part of a family of existing titles or needs to fit an established template, there may be limits on how far you can go with this; however, it is worth bearing these points in mind.

# 8 | Checklist of details to look out for

In addition to examining content, structure, clarity, tone and flow, the following is a suggested checklist of additional details to look out for. Developmental editors would usually be expected to try to resolve the points given below in Roman text themselves during the developmental edit, while they would flag those in dark blue for the author and/or publisher's attention (eg for the copyeditor at the next stage), either in the editorial report if one has been requested or by contacting them directly. However, where you draw the line between developmental and copyediting tasks will vary from edit to edit and will be influenced by the details of the brief.

## Abbreviations and consistency of terminology
- Does terminology fit the conventions of the field?
- Are abbreviations defined at first use?
- Are abbreviations defined consistently?
- Are abbreviations used too much?

## Presentation of data
- Are any data obviously missing or not adding up?
- Is too much or too little detail presented?
- Are important trends identified and described?
- Are data presented in a way that supports the development of the central argument or in order of decreasing importance?
- Are commas used for decimal points?
- Are numbers and units of measurement presented consistently?
- Are standard units of measurement used and given their proper abbreviations?

## Figures and tables
- Do all the tables and figures support the text in some way?
- Would any information in the text be better presented as a figure or table to aid the reader?
- Are there likely to be any issues relating to permissions?
- Are all tables and figures numbered, mentioned in the text and cited in order?
- Is all the relevant information provided (eg titles, scale bars, captions/legends, keys, etc)?
- Are all the figures of sufficient quality?

## Citations
- Is the frequency of reference citations consistent (ie does one chapter have a citation at the end of every sentence while another has almost none)?
- Are too many or too few references cited based on the content (ie are lots of references cited to support a point of common knowledge, or are large sections presented without any citations)?
- Are all quotes appropriately credited?
- Are all references cited in the list and vice versa?
- Are references listed consistently?

## Biased or insensitive language
- Is the language used inclusive and non-discriminatory?
- Are generalisations used that may offend the reader?
- If a medical or scientific text, is patient-first language used (ie 'a person with diabetes' not 'a diabetes patient', and 'participant' not 'subject')?

## Potential legal or ethical issues
- Do you suspect that any laws or ethical codes may have been infringed?
- Does any content appear to have been plagiarised?
- If the author is responsible for seeking copyright permissions to use images or quotes, have they done so?

# 9 | Resources

## Books and guides

Bacon, C (2020). *Editing Scientific and Medical Research Articles*. CIEP. This guide outlines the structural and stylistic elements required in scientific and medical research articles.

Cashmore, S (2020). *Proofreading Theses and Dissertations*. CIEP. This guide provides further information on what is and is not ethically acceptable when editing theses and dissertations.

Ginna, P (2017) (ed.). *What Editors Do: The art, craft, and business of book editing*. University of Chicago Press. This book contains several chapters written by different developmental editors that cover various aspects of their work and their experiences.

Norton, S (2009). *Developmental Editing: A handbook for freelancers, authors, and publishers*. University of Chicago Press. This book includes case studies that consider a variety of non-fiction texts and provides advice on how to approach developmental editing.

Saffrey, A (2020). *Editorial Project Management*. CIEP. This guide outlines principles of project management relating to editing.

Thompson, M (2020). *Pricing a Project: How to prepare a professional quotation*. CIEP. This guide outlines the quotation process, from taking a brief to agreeing terms and conditions.

## CIEP fact sheets and focus papers

Being aware of gendered language (available to members).

Editing LGBTQ+ language with sensitivity (available to members).

Editorial judgement (available to members).

The state of gendered language, by Sarah Grey (available to all).

What's in a name? Disability terminology for writers and editors, by Tom Shakespeare (available to all).

## Courses

Editors Canada provides a list of external courses that include structural editing and which match Editors Canada's specifications.

www.editors.ca/professional-development/education-and-additional-training-editors

Structural Editing Standards. A nine-week course offered by Queens' University, Canada, intended to serve as preparation for the Editors Canada Professional Certification test and recognised by the CIEP as counting towards CIEP membership upgrade. Developmental editing of both fiction and non-fiction are covered.

pros.educ.queensu.ca/courses/CONT204

Rewriting and Substantive Editing (Non-Fiction). A live course offered by the Publishing Training Centre that consists of four 90-minute sessions split into two half-day sessions, with exercises and feedback. Although rewriting and substantive editing are not the same as developmental editing, developmental editors may find the skills covered to be useful.

www.publishingtrainingcentre.co.uk/courses/virtual-classroom-courses/editorial-2/rewriting-and-substantive-editing-non-fiction

## Mentoring

The CIEP mentoring scheme is undergoing a full strategic review and will be relaunched in future.

www.ciep.uk/training/mentoring

Editors Canada offers the John Eerkes-Medrano Mentorship Program to members and student affiliates of Editors Canada.

www.editors.ca/professional-development/john-eerkes-medrano-mentorship-program

The Institute of Professional Editors Limited, the professional association for Australian and New Zealand editors, offers editors a mentoring programme through which editors can learn from other editors.

www.iped-editors.org/professional-development/iped-mentoring-program

## Blogs

There are some posts about developmental editing on the CIEP blog: **blog.ciep.uk**.

The Editors' Weekly blog also has some articles about non-fiction developmental editing: **blog.editors.ca/?tag=developmental-editing**.

Gary Smailes provides a comprehensive summary of what is required in developmental editing and the skills that non-fiction developmental editors need: **bubblecow.com/blog/developmental-editing-for-non-fiction**.

Bennett R Coles outlines why developmental editing is necessary for non-fiction books: **cascadiaauthorservices.com/developmental-editing**.

## Webinars

Academic Developmental Editing. Aimed at freelance editors looking to branch into developmental editing for academic clients, and for those who have academic writing experience but may be new to freelance editing.

www.the-efa.org/product/academic-developmental-editing-webinar-recording

Developmental Editing for Academics. Covers what developmental editing is and how it fits into the academic publishing process for journal and books.

courses.manuscriptworks.com/p/defa-webinar

Introduction to Developmental Editing. Outlines how developmental editing differs from copyediting, what developmental editors do and how to start honing your own developmental editing skills.

www.the-efa.org/product/introduction-to-developmental-editing-webinar-recording

# About the author

Claire Beveridge is a developmental editor, copyeditor and writer who specialises in non-fiction. She founded Beveridge Editorial Services in 2013 and is an Advanced Professional Member of the CIEP.

Claire has a PhD in cancer biochemistry, and has worked with numerous publishing companies and international organisations. In addition to done-for-you editing and copywriting services, she also offers coaching and training to other editors, and to business owners looking to increase the impact of their writing.

www.beveridgeeditorialservices.co.uk

## Acknowledgements

Thank you to everyone at the CIEP for giving me the opportunity to write this guide, particularly Cathy Tingle, Harriet Power, Julia Sandford-Cooke, Abi Saffrey and the reviewers for their helpful feedback. Special thanks go to Liz Dalby for her support and encouragement during the writing process.

www.ingramcontent.com/pod-product-compliance
Lightning Source LLC
Chambersburg PA
CBHW041311110526
44590CB00028B/4325